SOCIAL STUDIES

Skills REVIEW

WITH ANSWER KEY

HOLT, RINEHART AND **WINSTON**
Harcourt Brace & Company
Austin • New York • Orlando • Atlanta • San Francisco • Boston • Dallas • Toronto • London

Printed in the United States of America

ISBN 0-03-051979-9

8 9 10 11 085 04 03 02 01

TABLE OF CONTENTS

CRITICAL THINKING OVERVIEW

In all your Social Studies classes, you are asked to think critically about events and issues that have shaped United States and world history and that continue to shape society and life and the world around us. Thinking critically means using reason to judge information and ideas. People who have learned to think critically study information to determine its accuracy. They evaluate arguments and analyze conclusions before accepting them as valid or true. Critical thinkers have the ability to recognize and define problems and to develop plans and strategies for resolving those problems.

The development of critical thinking skills is essential to being an effective citizen. These skills help you to exercise your civic rights and responsibilities. For example, critical thinking skills assist you in logically judging the truth or honesty of political messages and in forming reasoned opinions about news reports. The ability to think critically enables you to be a smart voter and wise consumer.

Helping you to develop critical thinking skills is an important goal of all Holt, Rinehart and Winston Social Studies programs. The following 14 critical thinking skills provide a broad-based overview of what is needed to become a critical thinker. The skill lessons and worksheets that make up the *Skills Handbook* provide in-depth instruction in skills development and enable you to practice and apply various thinking skills.

USING HISTORICAL IMAGINATION

Using historical imagination means mentally stepping into the past to consider an event or situation as people at the time would have considered it. In putting yourself in their place, you might note whether they lived before or after historical turning points. For example, ask yourself these questions: Did these people live before or after important medical advances such as the discovery of penicillin? before or after technological advances such as the invention of the automobile? before or after World War II?

You will also find it helpful to keep in mind what the people of the time did and did not know. For example, to appreciate the experience of a soldier wounded in the Civil War, you need to understand that little was known at the time about the causes of disease and infection.

GAINING A MULTICULTURAL PERSPECTIVE

To gain a multicultural perspective means to take a broad view of events, people, and situations and consider them in ways that are fair and sensitive to all cultural groups. A multicultural perspective broadens your understanding of United States and world history while deepening your appreciation of the diversity that is found in the nation and in the world.

For instance, studying Native American cultures before the arrival of Christopher Columbus helps you understand that the Europeans did not "discover" the Americas. Rather, they found a land already settled by people with long histories and rich, well-established cultures.

RECOGNIZING POINT OF VIEW

Recognizing point of view involves identifying which factors influence the beliefs, attitudes, and opinions of an individual or a group. Factors such as age, gender, religion, race, education, and economic status help shape an individual's point of view.

This thinking skill helps you to understand why people and groups see things as they do, and why they often see things so differently. Being able to recognize point of view also reinforces and strengthens your understanding that people's views may change over time or with a change in circumstances. When a point of view is highly personal or based on unreasoned judgment, it is considered to be biased.

COMPARING AND CONTRASTING

Comparing and contrasting is the act of examining events, situations, or points of view for their similarities and differences. Comparing involves focusing on both what is similar and what is different. Contrasting involves focusing only on the differences.

For example, if you were asked to compare Irish and Chinese immigrants to the United States in the 1800s, you might point out that both groups of immigrants came to America to help build the transcontinental railroad but that the Chinese primarily worked between California and Utah while the Irish worked between Utah and Nebraska. In contrasting the two groups, you could mention that language and racial barriers generally were more of a problem for Chinese immigrants. Other factors you could focus on for comparison and contrast might include their reasons for coming to the United States, the family life of the two immigrant groups in the United States, and the groups' religious beliefs and practices.

IDENTIFYING CAUSE AND EFFECT

Identifying cause and effect is part of understanding the relationship between events. A cause is any action that leads to an event; the outcome of that action is an effect. Most events, however, have more than one cause and effect.

For example, the actions of both the North American colonists and the British government brought about the American Revolution, which in turn had many far-reaching effects. Being able to uncover the causes and the effects of an event provides you with a much deeper and richer understanding of it. This skill also helps you to recognize and understand social and historical context, the times and places in which historical events occurred and the people who made them happen.

ANALYZING

Analyzing is the process of breaking information down into its parts and examining how those parts work together. Analysis helps you to better understand how something works or how it came to be.

To analyze why the Bill of Rights was added to the U.S. Constitution, for instance, you might study the conflicts between Federalists and Antifederalists, the work of the delegates at the Constitutional Convention, and the struggle for the Constitution's ratification. You would then learn that Federalists and Antifederalists quarreled over the establishment of a strong central government and that this conflict almost prevented the Constitution's ratification. After supporters of the Constitution promised that a bill of rights would be added to the Constitution by later amendment, however, the Antifederalists voted for it, the Constitution was ratified and the new government got under way. The first order of business was passing the Bill of Rights—10 amendments to the U.S. Constitution that protect individual liberties and states' rights.

ASSESSING CONSEQUENCES

Assessing consequences involves studying an action, an event, or a trend to predict what its long-term effects or results will be, so we can judge how desirable those effects might be. Consequences are effects that are often not direct nor intended and may appear long after the event that led to them.

Developing the ability to assess consequences helps you to think beyond the present. This critical thinking skill also allows you to stretch your imagination and your thinking by identifying and considering more than one possibility. An example of assessing consequences is the federal government's weighing of the positive and negative outcomes of a new medication or medical procedure before allowing its use. Possible consequences include side effects and other risks, as well as any benefits to patients.

DISTINGUISHING FACT FROM OPINION

To distinguish fact from opinion means to separate information about a subject that can be verified from what people say about the subject. A fact can be proved or observed; an opinion, on the other hand, is a personal belief or conclusion. Thus, in an argument, opinions do not carry as much weight as facts, although some opinions can be supported by facts. Often you will hear facts and opinions mixed together in everyday conversation as well as in advertising, political debate, and historical sources.

Learning to separate fact from opinion and identify which is which helps you to critically evaluate information you read or are told. This thinking skill also teaches you how to strengthen your own arguments by supporting your opinions with facts.

IDENTIFYING VALUES

Identifying values means recognizing the core beliefs held by a person or group. Values are more deeply felt and more deeply held than opinions and thus are less likely to change. Values commonly center around issues of right and wrong and good and bad.

The values of freedom and justice, for example, caused people to struggle to abolish slavery in the United States, just as the value of equality has been a contributing factor in the nation's civil rights and women's movements. Being able to identify values helps you to understand why people and groups see things the way they do. It also helps you to understand your own personal view of the world.

HYPOTHESIZING

Hypothesizing involves forming a possible explanation for an event, a situation, or a problem. A hypothesis is not a proven fact. Rather it is an educated guess based on available evidence. Its truth or validity is tested by new evidence. A historian, for example, might hypothesize that the Civil War was chiefly the result of a power struggle between different economic and labor systems—the agricultural South versus the industrial North, slave versus free labor. The historian would organize facts to support this hypothesis and challenge the other explanations or hypotheses given for the causes of the Civil War.

Keep in mind that any hypothesis you offer about an event, a situation, or a problem should be based on the facts available to you, not on your opinions. Basing your hypothesis on facts lends it weight and forms a solid foundation against which you and possibly others can test its truth or validity.

SYNTHESIZING

To synthesize means to combine information and ideas from more than one source or points in time. Much of the narrative writing in your Social Studies textbooks is a synthesis of other material. Synthesizing allows you to combine the best of different materials to provide a broader and more in-depth look at a topic.

Synthesizing the history of the Great Depression, for example, might involve studying economic statistics and photographs from the 1930s, together with in-depth interviews of Americans who lived through the period. When you are asked to synthesize information or ideas, keep in mind that your goal should be to choose the best sources and blend and unify them into an easily understandable whole.

PROBLEM SOLVING

Problem solving is a process of examing and judging a situation, then making decisions and recommendations for improving or correcting it. Before seeking solutions, however, the problem must be identified and clearly stated. For instance, in considering a solution to the United States's drug abuse problem, you might state the problem in terms of the connection between drug addiction and violent crime. You would then suggest and evaluate possible solutions or courses of action to that problem, finally choosing the one you think is best and stating the reasons for your choice.

Learning to be an effective problem solver, helps you to identify and focus on what the real problem is, helps you critically judge the value of possible alternatives and solutions, makes you more aware of the issues and events in the world around you, and sharpens your leadership skills.

EVALUATING

Evaluating means considering and judging the significance or overall importance of something, such as the success of a reform movement or the record of a particular president. Whenever you are given an assignment to evaluate something, remember that you should base your judgment on standards that other people will understand and are likely to consider valid. An evaluation of the women's movement of the mid-1800s, for instance, might center around assessing what were the short-term and long-term effects of the movement's focus on winning the right to vote.

TAKING A STAND

To take a stand means to identify an issue, determine what you think about it, and persuasively express your position on the issue. Your position should be based on specific information. In taking a stand, even on controversial or emotional issues, state your position clearly and provide reasons to support it. Standing up for your beliefs may demand courage, but remember that if your argument is clear and well thought out, it will lend support to your position and help persuade people of its validity.

IDENTIFYING THE MAIN IDEA   **SKILL LESSON**

In all areas of Social Studies, significant events and ideas sometimes get lost among the many details. The ability to identify the main idea is a key to understanding any complex issue. Holt, Rinehart and Winston Social Studies textbooks are designed to help you to focus on these main ideas. Often these textbooks have introductory paragraphs and focus questions at the beginning of each chapter or section that are intended to guide your reading. Main ideas are sometimes highlighted at various places within the text to focus your attention on what is most important and to strengthen and reinforce your learning.

However, not everything you read is structured like a Holt, Rinehart and Winston Social Studies textbook. Applying the following guidelines will help you to identify the main ideas in other things you read.

HOW TO IDENTIFY THE MAIN IDEA

1. **Read introductory material.** Read the title and the introduction, if there is one. Often these identify the main ideas that will be discussed in the selection.

2. **Have questions in mind.** Before you read, think of questions about the topic that might be answered in the reading. Having questions in mind as you read the selection will help you to focus your reading.

3. **Note the outline of ideas.** Pay attention to any headings or subheadings in the selection that you read. They may provide you with a basic outline of the major ideas.

4. **Distinguish supporting details.** As you read the selection, distinguish sentences which provide supporting details from the general statements they support. A trail of facts may lead to the conclusion they support, and that conclusion may express a main idea.

PRACTICING YOUR SKILL

To practice your skill, read the paragraph below and then answer the questions that follow.

> Conflicts over religious principles had raged in England since 1534 when King Henry VIII broke away from the Roman Catholic Church to form the Church of England (Anglican Church). Henry's motives for the break had primarily been personal—the pope had refused to allow the king to divorce his first wife. Because he remained a Roman Catholic at heart, though, Henry had created a church that was still largely Catholic in form. This deeply distressed the Pilgrims, who yearned for a truly Protestant church.

1. Why is it important to have questions in mind as you read a selection?

2. Why is it important to follow the trail of facts provided in a selection?

3. What is the focus of the paragraph shown above? What is the paragraph's main idea?

4. What details lend support to the paragraph's main idea?

IDENTIFYING THE MAIN IDEA

SKILL WORKSHEET

APPLYING THE SKILL I

The following paragraph provides additional information about the Pilgrims. To identify the main idea, read the paragraph and then answer the questions that follow.

> The Pilgrims, known as Separatists because they had broken with the Church of England, left England for the more religiously tolerant Netherlands after receiving threats from King James I for their beliefs. In the Netherlands, however, the Pilgrims were forced to take low-paying, un-skilled jobs, coming face to face with the realities of poverty. Even more upsetting, they faced the possibility of losing control of their children. Not only were the children adopting Dutch ways, they also were being led, according to Pilgrim leader William Bradford, by the example of Dutch children into behaviors contrary to those set down for them by their parents and the other Pilgrims. Seeing life in the Netherlands as a threat to their financial well-being and to their way of life, Bradford and other Pilgrims sought and obtained permission to settle in Virginia.

1. What is the main idea of the paragraph? _____

_____

2. What details support the main idea? _____

_____

3. Reread the paragraph on page 5 concerning the Church of England. What is the relationship of the main ideas of the paragraph above and the paragraph on page 5? Write a statement that summarizes the information in both paragraphs.

_____

_____

_____

APPLYING THE SKILL II

With the approval of your teacher, choose a topic about which you have a strong basic knowledge. In the space below, write a paragraph about that topic. Then, identify the main idea of your paragraph and the details that support the main idea.

_____

_____

_____

_____

Main Idea: _____

Supporting Details: _____

IDENTIFYING CAUSE AND EFFECT   SKILL LESSON

Identifying and understanding cause-and-effect relationships is an important Social Studies skill. To learn why an event took place and what happened as a result of that event, social scientists ask questions such as these: What was the immediate action that triggered the event? What was the background leading up to the event? Who were the people involved? Your task is simpler than the social scientist's—you only need to trace what we already know about the connection of actions and outcomes.

HOW TO IDENTIFY CAUSE AND EFFECT

1. **Be alert to clues.** Certain words and phrases are clues to the existence of a cause-and-effect relationship. Study the examples in the box at the right.
2. **Identify the relationship.** Read carefully to identify how events are related. Writers do not always state the link between cause and effect. Sometimes a reader must judge the cause or the effect.
3. **Check for complex connections.** Beyond the immediate or superficial cause and effect, check for other, less obvious, more complex connections. Note, for instance, whether there were other causes of a given effect, whether a cause had multiple effects, and whether these effects themselves caused further events.

CLUE WORDS AND PHRASES	
Cause	**Effect**
as a result of	aftermath
because	as a consequence
brought about	depended on
inspired	gave rise to
led to	originating from
produced	outcome
provoked	outgrowth
spurred	proceeded from
the reason	resulting in

PRACTICING YOUR SKILL

To practice your skill, complete the activities that follow.

1. Among the events leading up to the American Revolution was the British government's taxing its colonies to help pay the debt incurred in the French and Indian War. Diagram this relationship by choosing and writing the correct sentence below on the proper set of lines.

   Parliament levies taxes on the colonies.
   Britain incurs a huge debt while fighting the French and Indian War.

   Cause   **Effect**

   _____   _____
                          ⟶
   _____   _____

2. Parliament's taxation of the colonies to pay its debt led the colonists to exclaim, "No taxation without representation." Diagram this complex relationship below and show how an effect may become a cause by writing each sentence on the proper set of lines.

   Colonists protest taxation without representation.
   Britain incurs a huge debt while fighting the French and Indian War.
   Parliament levies taxes on the colonies.

   Cause   **Effect/Cause**   **Effect**

   _____   _____   _____

   _____   _____   _____
                  ⟶   ⟶
   _____   _____   _____

   _____   _____   _____

IDENTIFYING CAUSE AND EFFECT

SKILL WORKSHEET

APPLYING THE SKILL I

The following questions focus on the steps involved in identifying cause-and-effect relationships. To check your understanding of these steps, answer the questions in the space provided.

1. When reading about an event, why is it sometimes necessary to judge what is a cause or an effect?

   _____

2. What three things might complex relationships have that simple ones do not? _____

   _____

3. List two words or phrases that may serve as clues to a cause and two words or phrases that may serve as clues to an effect. (Note: Do not use the examples shown in the chart on page 7.)

   Cause: _____

   Effect: _____

APPLYING THE SKILL II

In each of the following pairs, one event or circumstance is the cause, and the other its effect. Mark an *X* on the line in front of the sentence that contains the cause.

1. _____ a. Henry Bessemer developed a steel-making method that could produce more steel in a day than other methods could produce in a week.

   _____ b. Skyscrapers and mass transit transformed U.S. cities.

2. _____ a. The United States fought against the Axis Powers in World War II.

   _____ b. The Japanese bombed Pearl Harbor on December 7, 1941.

3. _____ a. The Eighteenth Amendment banned the manufacture, sale, and importation of alcoholic beverages.

   _____ b. During the Progressive Era, many people wanted to "clean up" what they considered to be immoral behavior.

4. _____ a. The Great Depression was the most serious economic downturn the United States had ever experienced.

   _____ b. Panicked by the 1929 stock market crash, many Americans waited in long lines to withdraw their money from U.S. banks.

5. _____ a. Mikhail Gorbachev's efforts to reform the Soviet Union included instituting the new policies of freedom, glasnost and perestroika.

   _____ b. The Cold War ended.

6. _____ a. During the 1992 presidential campaign, many Americans expressed dissatisfaction with "politics as usual."

   _____ b. Ross Perot had the strongest showing of any third-party presidential candidate since Theodore Roosevelt.

Social Studies Skills Review

STUDYING PRIMARY AND SECONDARY SOURCES   SKILL LESSON

There are many sources of firsthand information, including diaries, letters, editorials, speeches, and legal documents such as wills and property titles. All of these are primary sources. Other primary sources include newspaper articles, generally written after the fact, and autobiographies and personal memoirs, images which are usually written late in a person's life. Visual images such as photographs, paintings, and political cartoons also are primary sources. Because they provide a way to understand more directly what people of the time were thinking, primary sources are valuable tools.

Secondary sources also are descriptions or interpretations of events, but they are written after the events have taken place and by people who did not witness the events. Examples of secondary sources include history textbooks, biographies, encyclopedias, and other reference works. Writers of secondary sources have the advantage of being able to see what happened after the time period being studied. Thus they can provide a wider perspective than a participant or witness to an event can.

HOW TO STUDY PRIMARY AND SECONDARY SOURCES

1. **Examine the material carefully.** Consider the nature of the source material. Is it verbal or visual? Is it based on firsthand information or on the accounts of others? Pay attention to the major ideas and the supporting details.
2. **Consider the audience.** Ask yourself this question: For whom was this message originally intended? Whether a message was meant, for instance, for the general public or for a specific, private audience may have shaped the message's style or content.
3. **Be alert to bias.** Watch for words or phrases that present a one-sided or slanted view of a person or event.
4. **When possible, compare sources.** Try to examine more than one source on a given topic. Comparing sources gives you a more complete, balanced account of people and events and their connections.
5. **Draw conclusions.** Use your careful reading of the source material to draw conclusions about the event or topic discussed.

PRACTICING YOUR SKILL

To practice your skill, read the passage below, which is part of the Farewell Address given by President George Washington as he was about to leave office in 1796. Then answer the questions that follow.

> The great rule of conduct for us in regard to foreign nations is, in extending our commercial [trade] relations to have with them as little *political* connection as possible. So far as we have already formed engagements let them be fulfilled with perfect good faith. Here let us stop.
>
> Europe has a set of primary interests which to us have none or a very remote relation. Hence she must be engaged in frequent controversies, the causes of which are essentially foreign to our concerns. Hence, therefore, it must be unwise in us to implicate [entangle] ourselves by artificial ties in the ordinary vicissitudes [ups and downs] of her politics or the ordinary combinations and collisions of her friendships or enmities [hostilities]. . . .
>
> It is our true policy to steer clear of permanent alliances with any portion of the foreign world.

1. Is the passage a primary source or a secondary source? Why?
2. What is the basic message of this portion of Washington's Farewell Address?
3. For what audience was this speech intended?
4. Why might Washington's Farewell Address be a good source of information about early U.S. foreign policy?

Social Studies Skills Review   **9**

STUDYING PRIMARY AND SECONDARY SOURCES   SKILL WORKSHEET

APPLYING THE SKILL I

The items listed below are examples of primary and secondary sources. Write *P* for each primary source and *S* for each secondary source.

_____ **1.** a newspaper article

_____ **2.** a private journal

_____ **3.** a biography

_____ **4.** an editorial cartoon

_____ **5.** a medieval tapestry

_____ **6.** a textbook on the history of Asia

_____ **7.** a photograph of a family vacation

_____ **8.** a magazine article on the history of Texas

_____ **9.** an autobiography

_____ **10.** a property deed

APPLYING THE SKILL II

The following is an excerpt from the Declaration of Independence, which was written by Thomas Jefferson to explain why the American colonies wanted to break away from British control. To apply your skill, read the excerpt and then answer the questions that follow.

> When in the Course of human events it becomes necessary for one people to dissolve [break] the political bands which have connected them with another, and to assume among the powers of the earth, the separate and equal station to which the Laws of Nature and of Nature's God entitle them, a decent respect to the opinions of mankind requires that they should declare the causes which impel [drive] them to the separation.—
>
> We hold these truths to be self-evident, that all men are created equal, that they are endowed [provided] by their Creator with certain unalienable [permanent] Rights, that among these are Life, Liberty and the Pursuit of Happiness.—That to secure these rights, Governments are instituted among Men, deriving [receiving] their just powers from the consent of the governed,— That whenever any Form of Government becomes destructive of these ends, it is the Right of the People to alter or to abolish [end] it, and to institute new Government, laying its foundation on such principles, and organizing its powers in such form, as to them shall seem most likely to effect their Safety and Happiness.

1. Why is the Declaration of Independence a primary source? _____

_____

2. What is the purpose of the first paragraph? _____

_____

3. To what rights are all people entitled, according to this excerpt? _____

_____

Social Studies Skills Review

BUILDING YOUR VOCABULARY   SKILL LESSON

Reading Social Studies textbooks may challenge your understanding. You will probably find many new and unfamiliar words along the way. With a systematic plan and regular effort, however, you can increase your understanding and comprehension of the material and turn reading Social Studies into an opportunity to enlarge your vocabulary. In addition, you will find that mastering unfamiliar words helps not only in your studies but also in conversation and in any outside reading that you do. Following the steps outlined below will help you in building your vocabulary.

HOW TO BUILD YOUR VOCABULARY

1. **Identify unfamiliar words.** As you read your textbook or any other materials, be aware of words that you cannot pronounce or define. Make and keep a list of these words. You will find that words that are somewhat familiar to you are the easiest words to learn.

2. **Study context clues.** Carefully examine the sentence and paragraph in which you find the new word. The other words, or context, may give you clues to the unfamiliar word's meaning. Another more familiar word that means the same thing may be used in the same sentence or paragraph, or an example of what the word means may be given.

3. **Use a dictionary and a thesaurus.** Use a dictionary to learn how to pronounce and define the words on your list. You can further familiarize yourself with the words by using a thesaurus to find synonyms for them.

4. **Review new vocabulary.** Be sure to write down the definition of each word you look up in the dictionary. Take every opportunity to review the words and their definitions until you feel comfortable with them. Consider making a set of flash cards to use for review purposes. Ask a friend or family member to test you on the words.

5. **Use new vocabulary.** Look for ways to use the new words—in homework assignments, in conversation, or in classroom discussions. The best way to master a new word is to use it.

PRACTICING YOUR SKILL

To practice your skill, answer the questions and complete the activity that follows.

1. What is context? How can context provide clues to a word's meaning?

2. Why is it important to use a dictionary when you come across unfamiliar words?

3. How can using a thesaurus help you to build your vocabulary?

4. Why is it important to look for opportunities to use the new words you have learned?

5. Read a chapter from your Social Studies textbook, listing any unfamiliar words that you find. Write down what you think each word means, and then check your definitions against those in a dictionary. Create an effective plan for committing those words to memory.

BUILDING YOUR VOCABULARY

APPLYING THE SKILL I

The following words and definitions are important in the study of history. Refer to a dictionary or history textbook and match each definition on the left with the correct word on the right by writing the letter of the term in the space provided.

_____ 1. person who lived on a feudal manor and worked the feudal lord's land in exchange for crops and protection

_____ 2. person who wanted to put an end to the institution of slavery

a. conquistador
b. peon
c. escalation
d. abolitionist
e. serf
f. détente

_____ 3. lessening of diplomatic and military tensions between nations

_____ 4. Spanish soldier who helped conquer the Americas

_____ 5. buildup of military forces or weapons

_____ 6. landless laborer, usually an American Indian, who worked on a Spanish hacienda

APPLYING THE SKILL II

Refer to a dictionary or textbook and complete each sentence by writing the appropriate term from the list below.

electors	depression	urban renewal	ecosystem
segregation	veto	carpetbaggers	utopia

1. In an _____, living beings interact with their environment.

2. The power to reject a proposed law is called a(n) _____.

3. An ideal community is a(n) _____.

4. _____ are people chosen by state legislatures to cast electoral votes for the president and vice president.

5. A(n) _____ is a sharp drop in profits and business activity accompanied by rising unemployment.

6. The term for northern Republicans who moved to the South after the Civil War to help freedpeople or to seek financial gain is _____.

7. The forced separation of the races is known as _____.

8. _____ is a type of program designed to replace or restore run-down inner-city buildings.

Social Studies Skills Review

DISTINGUISHING FACT FROM OPINION   SKILL LESSON

One of the keys to evaluating what you read and hear is the ability to distinguish fact from opinion. A fact is something that can be proved true. Facts can be counted, measured, or verified in some way. Opinions, on the other hand, are personal beliefs about what is true. Because people often use facts to support their opinions, it is important to know how to distinguish between the two. Once you have learned this skill, you will be better able to evaluate the information you read and hear on a daily basis.

HOW TO DISTINGUISH FACT FROM OPINION

1. **Determine if the information can be proved.** You can begin to identify facts by asking the same questions a journalist uses to write a good newspaper article. If the information answers the questions *Who? What? When? Where? Why?* and *How?* it probably contains facts. Next, determine if the facts can be documented, perhaps in sources such as almanacs or encyclopedias. Facts can be checked and verified, but opinions cannot.

2. **Pay attention to how the facts are used.** Note that a single word often can change a statement from fact to opinion. Certain phrases, such as "I think that . . . ," "I believe that . . . ," and "In my judgment . . . ," are a clear signal that the writer or speaker is about to give an opinion.

3. **Identify "loaded" words.** Loaded words are words that contain an emotional appeal. Examples of loaded words are *exciting, beautiful, boring,* and *extremely.* These descriptive words signal an opinion because they express the writer's or speaker's personal point of view. Do not permit loaded words to influence your judgment of the facts.

PRACTICING YOUR SKILL

To practice your skill, examine the election campaign flier below. Then answer the questions that follow.

TERESA ORTEGA *for* CITY COUNCIL

Teresa Ortega is determined to make our city a better place to live. If elected, Ortega will

- guarantee that our city taxes are fair and reasonable. Over the past 10 years, our city taxes have been increased four times.
- expand the number of city buses available during rush hour. Currently, 25 percent of our public buses do not operate during rush hour.
- add to and improve facilities for older citizens. At present, more than 200 of our older citizens are waiting to participate in city-run programs.

Teresa Ortega knows our city well. She is a dedicated, hardworking educator who has served successfully on the school board for more than 10 years.

ELECT TERESA ORTEGA
She will make our city a better place to live.

---

1. Identify the loaded words in the following sentence: "She is a dedicated, hardworking educator who has served successfully on the school board for more than 10 years." How might these loaded words influence people's interpretation of the facts?

2. Imagine that you are a journalist for a local newspaper. Which facts from the campaign flier would you include in your news article?

DISTINGUISHING FACT FROM OPINION   **SKILL WORKSHEET**

APPLYING THE SKILL I

Read each of the statements below. Then in the space provided, write *F* if the statement is a fact and *O* if the statement is an opinion.

_____ **1.** Abraham Lincoln was the sixteenth president of the United States.

_____ **2.** Joining the Peace Corps is the best way for someone to help people in need.

_____ **3.** Mayan pottery is the most beautiful pottery ever made.

_____ **4.** The two major U.S. political parties are the Democratic Party and the Republican Party.

_____ **5.** Patriotism is the strongest emotion people can feel.

_____ **6.** The best movies were produced during the 1970s.

_____ **7.** Albert Einstein developed the special theory of relativity.

_____ **8.** Congress adopted the final draft of the Declaration of Independence on July 4, 1776.

_____ **9.** The United States was right to participate in the Persian Gulf War.

_____ **10.** Lee Harvey Oswald was arrested for the assassination of President John F. Kennedy.

APPLYING THE SKILL II

For each topic listed below, write one statement based on fact and one statement based on opinion. Consult a Social Studies textbook or a reference book for background information, if needed.

1. The 1996 Presidential Election

   Fact: _____

   Opinion: _____

2. Christopher Columbus

   Fact: _____

   Opinion: _____

3. The Civil War

   Fact: _____

   Opinion: _____

4. The Constitution of the United States

   Fact: _____

   Opinion: _____

5. Your Home State

   Fact: _____

   Opinion: _____

FORMING GENERALIZATIONS   SKILL LESSON

Textbooks contain thousands of facts. Because there are so many facts, it is sometimes difficult to understand how they relate to one another and what their underlying meaning might be. One way to synthesize, or combine, a group of facts is to form generalizations. A generalization is a broad statement that describes a situation in terms of what is generally true. Most generalizations are used to connect different facts about the same situation or topic. The steps outlined below will help you to form generalizations.

HOW TO FORM GENERALIZATIONS

1. **Collect information about the topic.** As you read your textbook or other material, gather as many facts as you can about a particular topic or event. Make sure the facts come from trustworthy sources. Although you can be sure that all of the facts presented in textbooks published by Holt, Rinehart and Winston have been checked and verified, this is not always true of everything you read or hear. If the facts are incorrect, your general statement about the facts will be incorrect.

2. **Look for relationships among the facts.** Ask yourself what the facts have in common and what links them. Determine if the evidence forms a pattern. For example, the statements "Hank likes spaghetti," "Hank likes lasagna," and "Hank likes ravioli" are related in that they concern foods that Hank likes and that those foods are types of pasta. Thus the evidence forms a pattern.

3. **Form a general statement about the related facts.** Remember that when forming a generalization, all of the specific evidence must lead to the same general conclusion. If any of the facts do not fit, the generalization will not be correct. For example, knowing that Hank likes spaghetti, lasagna, and ravioli could lead you to make the general statement that Hank likes pasta. If you know, however, that Hank likes lasagna and ravioli but hates spaghetti, you could not make the same generalization.

4. **Make sure your generalization is valid.** Keep in mind that your generalization must take into account all of the facts but must not make claims that the facts do not support. For example, if you hear a loud crash and the screech of metal, see a group of people gathering in the street, and then hear the siren of an approaching ambulance, you could use these facts to make the general statement that an accident has occurred. You could not, however, use these facts to say that there has been an accident involving an automobile and a motorcycle.

PRACTICING YOUR SKILL

To practice your skill, answer the questions and complete the activities that follow.

1. When forming a generalization, why is it important that all of the evidence lead to the same conclusion?

2. How can you determine if your generalization is valid?

3. Form a generalization based on the three statements below.
   • There are no cars in the school parking lot.
   • All of the school doors are locked.
   • There are no lights on in the school.

4. Determine which of the three statements below is a generalization.
   • Changes in technology affect the kinds of jobs available to workers.
   • In industry, automation has decreased the need for unskilled workers.
   • Improvements in farming technology have made it possible to grow more food using fewer workers.

FORMING GENERALIZATIONS

APPLYING THE SKILL I

Identify which statement in each set is a generalization by marking an *X* in the space provided.

1. _____ **a.** The sky is getting dark.

   _____ **b.** A storm is coming.

   _____ **c.** The temperature is dropping.

   _____ **d.** Clouds are forming.

2. _____ **a.** There are newspapers in the yard.

   _____ **b.** The house is dark.

   _____ **c.** The residents are on vacation.

   _____ **d.** No cars are in the driveway.

3. _____ **a.** Americans enjoy many rights and freedoms.

   _____ **b.** Americans have the right to criticize their government officials.

   _____ **c.** No one has the right to force a U.S. citizen to vote for a particular candidate.

   _____ **d.** Freedom of the press is guaranteed by the U.S. Constitution.

APPLYING THE SKILL II

In the space provided, write a generalization for each of the following sets of statements.

1. • When more than 5,000 U.S. banks failed in the early 1930s, many people lost their life savings.
   • During the Great Depression, many people waited in breadlines for bowls of soup and pieces of bread.
   • By 1932 about 12 million Americans were unemployed.

   Generalization: _____

   _____

   _____

2. • The wealthiest 20 percent of the U.S. population controls about three fourths of the nation's assets.
   • Nearly half of the total income of all Americans is earned by the richest 20 percent of the U.S. population.
   • It is estimated that the top U.S. corporate executives earn 100 times as much money as the lowest-paid production workers.

   Generalization: _____

   _____

   _____

DOING LIBRARY RESEARCH

SKILL LESSON

To complete research papers or special projects, you may need to use resources other than your textbook. For instance, you may want to research specific topics or people not discussed in the textbook, or you may want to obtain additional information about a particular topic. Doing such research involves using the resources available in a library or media center.

HOW TO FIND INFORMATION

To find a particular book, you need to understand how libraries organize their materials. Usually fiction books are alphabetized according to the last name of the author. Libraries classify nonfiction books by using the Dewey decimal system or the Library of Congress system. Both systems assign each book a call number that tells you the book's location.

To find the call number of a book, look in the library's card catalog. The card catalog lists books by author, by title, and by subject. If you know the author or title of the book, finding it is easy. If you only know the book's subject, or if you simply want to find any book on a subject, look up that subject heading. Many libraries now have computerized card catalogs. Such catalogs generally contain the same information as traditional card catalogs, but take up less space and are easier to update and use.

Librarians can help you to use the card catalog and direct you to a book's location. They also can suggest additional resources and answer questions about how material is organized in the library. Many libraries now rely on computerized resources.

HOW TO USE LIBRARY RESOURCES

In a library's reference section, you will find many useful resources such as encyclopedias, specialized dictionaries, atlases, almanacs, and indexes to recent material in magazines and newspapers. Encyclopedias often will prove to be your best resource. Encyclopedias include biographical sketches of notable historical figures; economic, political, and geographic information on individual nations, states, and cities; discussions of historical events and religious, social, and cultural issues; and much more. Encyclopedia entries often include cross-references to related articles.

Specialized dictionaries are available for almost every field. A biographical dictionary has entries about many more people than does an encyclopedia. A historical dictionary includes definitions of historical terms as well as brief descriptions of such events as important laws, landmark court cases, and social movements.

A gazetteer is a geographical dictionary that lists important natural physical features and place-names. Pronunciation guides, statistical information, and brief descriptions also are included. An atlas contains maps and visual representations of geographic data.

To locate up-to-date facts about a topic, you can use almanacs, yearbooks, and periodical indexes. References such as *The World Almanac and Book of Facts* include historical information and a variety of statistics about such topics as population, the environment, and sports. Encyclopedia yearbooks provide up-to-date entries on new, important developments that are not discussed in the encyclopedia. Periodical indexes, in particular the *Readers' Guide to Periodical Literature,* can help you to find informative, current articles published in magazines. *The New York Times Index* catalogs the news articles published in the *Times,* a U.S. daily newspaper with in-depth coverage of national and world events.

PRACTICING YOUR SKILL

To practice your skill, answer the following questions.
1. How are nonfiction books classified?
2. What types of information can you get from the card catalog?
3. Which types of reference books contain information about geography?
4. Where would you look to locate the most recent coverage of a political or social issue?

DOING LIBRARY RESEARCH   SKILL WORKSHEET

APPLYING THE SKILL I

The following items are examples of the types of information that can be found in library reference books. Examine each item. Then in the space provided, identify which reference book or books you would look in to find the information.

1. number of arson cases in the United States in 1997: _____

2. Billy the Kid's real name: _____

3. history of the criminal justice system: _____

4. magazine articles on the most recent presidential election: _____

5. latitude of Bombay, India: _____

6. proper pronunciation of the former Soviet republic of Belarus: _____

7. biographical sketch of Susan B. Anthony: _____

8. purpose of the Taft-Hartley Act: _____

APPLYING THE SKILL II

The card below is an example of the types of information about a book that can be found in the library card catalog. Examine the card. Then answer the questions that follow.

> The Student's Guide to Fascinating U.S. History Facts.
>
> 973.02
> DOE   Doe, John, 1953–
>   The Student's Guide to Fascinating U.S.
>   History Facts / John Doe—New York: The
>   Superior Publishing Company, 1997.
>   xiv, 436 pp. 21cm.
>
>   Includes Bibliography and Index.
>
>   1. United States—History—Miscellanea.
>   I. Title. II. Title: The Student's Guide to
>   Fascinating U.S. History Facts.

1. What is the title of the book? _____

2. Who is the author of the book? _____

3. In what year was the book published? _____

4. Who is the publisher of the book? _____

5. How many pages does the book contain? _____

6. What is the book's call number? _____

CREATING AN OUTLINE

SKILL LESSON

An outline is a tool for organizing information and creating one is an important step in your preparation for writing. An outline includes the main ideas of what you have read or plan to communicate, and underneath them lists the details that support the main ideas. Remember, though, that an outline is only a framework—the essay you write from it must be fleshed out. But if you make sure that your outline is thorough and well thought out, writing the final product will be much easier.

HOW TO CREATE AN OUTLINE

1. **Order your material.** Decide what information you want to emphasize. Order or classify your material with that in mind. Then determine what information belongs in an introduction, what should make up the body of the essay or report, and what should be left for the conclusion.
2. **Identify main ideas.** Identify the main ideas to be presented in each section and use these ideas as your outline's main headings.
3. **List supporting details.** Determine what important details or facts support each main idea. Rank and list these details as subheadings under each main idea, using more levels of subheadings as needed. Keep in mind that you must have at least two entries under each subheading: no *A*'s without *B*'s, no *1*'s without *2*'s, no *a*'s without *b*'s.
4. **Put your outline to use.** Organize your essay or report according to your finished outline. Each main heading in the outline, for example, might form the basis for a topic sentence to begin a paragraph. Subheadings would then make up the content of the paragraph. In a more lengthy paper, each subheading might be the main idea of a paragraph.

PRACTICING YOUR SKILL

To practice your skill, examine the outline below, which could be used in preparation for writing about the Louisiana Purchase. Notice the several levels of headings that make up the various parts of the outline. Then answer the questions that follow.

> I. Republicans' support of westward expansion
>   A. Settlement of the Trans-Appalachian West
>   B. Access to the Mississippi River
>   1. Significance of the port of New Orleans
>   2. Spain's returning Louisiana to France
>   a. Threat to U.S. trade
>   b. Barrier to U.S. expansion westward
> II. President Jefferson's negotiations with France
>   A. America's purchase of Louisiana
>   B. Why France sold Louisiana
>   1. Napoleon's failure to build empire in the Americas
>   a. Need for naval base in West Indies
>   b. Revolt in Saint Domingue (now Haiti)
>   c. French failure to regain control of Haiti
>   2. Napoleon's need of money for war plans

1. How many levels of headings are included in the outline above?
2. What are the two main ideas contained in the outline?
3. Why did the fact that France regained control of Louisiana cause the United States concern?
4. For what two reasons did France decide to sell Louisiana to the United States?

CREATING AN OUTLINE

SKILL WORKSHEET

APPLYING THE SKILL I

The items listed below in the left column, when listed in the proper order, make up a two-level outline that could be used in preparation for writing about poverty in the United States. Use the right column to place these items in their correct outline order.

1. D. Single-parent families

2. IV. Programs to ease poverty

3. A. Unskilled workers

4. III. Effects of poverty

5. A. Government programs

6. I. Introduction/purpose

7. B. Volunteer programs

8. B. Racial and ethnic groups

9. V. Summary/conclusions

10. C. Self-esteem

11. C. Older Americans

12. A. Health

13. II. Who lives in poverty?

14. B. Education

1. _____

2. _____

3. _____

4. _____

5. _____

6. _____

7. _____

8. _____

9. _____

10. _____

11. _____

12. _____

13. _____

14. _____

APPLYING THE SKILL II

With the approval of your teacher, choose a subsection of a chapter in your Social Studies textbook to read. After you have read the subsection, use the space below, a separate sheet of paper, or a computer to create an outline of the information.

_____

_____

_____

_____

_____

_____

_____

🌐 WRITING ABOUT SOCIAL STUDIES   SKILL LESSON

Holt, Rinehart and Winston Social Studies textbooks provide you with numerous writing opportunities. Section Reviews often have writing exercises that give you the chance to write about a topic with a particular focus in mind. Chapter Reviews provide additional opportunities for writing.

WRITING WITH A PURPOSE

Always keep in mind your purpose for writing. That purpose might be to express a point of view, evaluate, synthesize, analyze, persuade, inform, or hypothesize. As you begin, your purpose for writing will determine the most appropriate approach to take; when you have completed, your purpose for writing will help you to evaluate your success.

Each different purpose for writing requires its own form, tone, and content. The point of view you are adopting will also shape what you write, and in addition you must shape your work to fit your intended audience, or whoever will be reading what you write. For example, the tone you would take when writing to the president of the United States would differ greatly from the tone you would take when writing to a pen pal.

USING HISTORICAL IMAGINATION

Many of the writing opportunities you will encounter in Social Studies require you to create a specific type of writing—for instance, a diary entry, a letter, a newspaper editorial, a poem, or an advertisement. Often such writing involves using historical imagination—that is, writing from the perspective of a person living then, rather than now.

An assignment may require, for example, that you address a particular historical figure, such as a former president, or that you write as if you were living through a specific historical event. When given such an assignment, try to imagine what people at the time would have experienced and what they might have thought or said about a particular circumstance or event.

The following guidelines address specific kinds of writing:

- A diary is an informal, personal record of your experiences and remembrances (or those of someone else in history). Entries are dated and consist of brief accounts of the day's happenings and your reactions to them.
- A letter is a personal communication intended for a specific individual.
- A newspaper editorial is a public statement of an opinion or a point of view. It takes a stand on a particular topic or issue and provides reasons for that stand.
- An advertisement is an announcement to promote a product or event. Effective advertisements are direct and to the point and use memorable language, such as slogans and jingles, to emphasize significant features of the product.

HOW TO WRITE A PAPER OR ESSAY

Each writing opportunity you encounter will have specific instructions about what and how to write. But whether you are writing a diary entry describing your experiences as a soldier during the Persian Gulf War or an essay about changes in military technology, you should follow certain basic steps.

Writing a paper or essay involves the following four major stages: prewriting, writing a first draft, evaluating and revising your draft, and proofreading and producing a final draft for publication. Each of these stages can be further divided into more specific steps and tasks. By using the following guidelines for each of these four stages, you can improve your writing abilities and produce more accurate and interesting writing assignments.

PREWRITING

1. **Select a topic.** Choose a topic for your paper or essay. Whenever possible, select a topic that is of interest to you. Be sure that you narrow your topic so that you will be able to develop and support a clear argument.

2. **Identify your purpose for writing.** Read the instructions carefully to identify the purpose for your writing. Let the purpose of the assignment guide you as you plan and write your paper or essay.

3. **Determine your intended audience.** When writing for a particular audience, be sure to adopt the tone and style that will best communicate your message.

4. **Collect information.** Jot down your ideas and the information you already know about your topic; then conduct additional research as necessary. Your writing process will be more efficient and well organized if you have many details at hand and know what information you still need.

5. **Create an outline.** Allow yourself sufficient time to think and plan before you begin writing your first draft. Organize themes, main ideas, and supporting details into an outline. This outline will help you to stay focused as you write so that you do not forget to include important information or add unnecessary details.

WRITING THE FIRST DRAFT

6. **Write a first draft and evaluate it.** In writing your first draft, remember to use your outline as a guide. Each paragraph should express a single main idea or set of related ideas and include details for support. Take care to show the relationships between ideas and to make proper use of transitions, which are sentences that establish connections between the paragraphs.

EVALUATING AND REVISING THE DRAFT

7. **Review and edit.** Revise and reorganize your first draft as needed to make your points. Refine dull or weak sentences by adding appropriate adjectives and adverbs. Delete any words, sentences, or paragraphs that are unnecessary, that are unrelated to a main idea, or that wander too far from a main point.

8. **Evaluate your writing style.** Clarify and strengthen your writing by changing the structure of awkward sentences. Replace vague or unclear words with more precise word choices.

PROOFREADING AND PUBLISHING

9. **Proofread your paper or essay carefully.** Check your work for proper spelling, punctuation, and grammar. Make any other minor changes that are necessary.

10. **Write your final version.** Prepare a neat final version. Appearance is important; it may not affect the quality of your work itself, but it can affect the way your work is perceived by others.

PRACTICING YOUR SKILL

To practice your skill, answer the following questions.

1. What factor, more than any other, should affect how and what you write? Why?

2. Why is it important to consider the intended audience for your writing?

3. What types of things should you do when editing the first draft of a writing assignment?

4. Why is it important to prepare a neat final version of a writing assignment?

WRITING ABOUT SOCIAL STUDIES   **SKILL WORKSHEET**

APPLYING THE SKILL I

The four sections contained in this skill worksheet provide you the opportunity to work through the four main stages in writing an essay. In this section, you will complete the steps involved in the prewriting stage. First, with the approval of your teacher, select a topic for your essay. Then, collect the information you will need to write your essay. Finally, on a separate sheet of paper, create an outline that will guide your writing. Use the checklist below to ensure that you complete all the necessary tasks. As you complete each task, place a check mark in the space provided.

_____ **1.** Topic selected

My topic is _____.

_____ **2.** Purpose of writing identified

My purpose is _____.

_____ **3.** Audience determined

My audience is _____.

_____ **4.** Information collected

_____ **5.** Outline completed

APPLYING THE SKILL II

In this section, you will complete the second stage involved in writing an essay—writing the first draft. Use the space below or a separate sheet of paper to write the draft. Remember to use your completed outline as a guide.

_____

_____

_____

_____

_____

_____

_____

_____

_____

_____

_____

APPLYING THE SKILL III

In this section, you will complete the third stage involved in writing an essay—evaluating and revising your first draft. On a separate sheet of paper, review and edit your draft and evaluate your writing style. Use the checklist below to ensure that you complete all the necessary tasks. As you complete each task, place a check mark in the space provided.

_____ **1.** Draft revised and reorganized to strengthen main points

_____ **2.** Sentences refined by adding appropriate adjectives and adverbs

_____ **3.** Unnecessary or unrelated words, sentences, and paragraphs deleted

_____ **4.** Awkward sentences clarified

_____ **5.** Ambiguous wording replaced

APPLYING THE SKILL IV

After you have checked your work for proper spelling, punctuation, and grammar, use the space below, a separate sheet of paper, or a computer to write the final version of your essay.

_____

_____

_____

_____

_____

_____

_____

_____

_____

_____

_____

_____

_____

_____

_____

_____

TAKING A TEST

SKILL LESSON

When it comes to taking a test, for Social Studies or for any other subject, nothing can take the place of preparation. A good night's sleep and consistent study habits give you a much better chance for success than do hours of late-night, last-minute cramming. In addition, you will find that being well prepared helps you to ignore any distractions that might occur during the test.

However, keeping your attention focused on the test and your mind free from distractions is not all you can do to improve your test scores. Mastering some basic test-taking skills can also help. Keeping up with daily reading assignments and taking careful notes as you read can make preparing for a test into a simple matter of review. Reviewing information that you already know takes less time—and causes less stress—than trying to learn something new under pressure.

You will face several basic types of questions on the tests you encounter—for example, fill in the blank, short answer, multiple choice, matching, and essay. In answering multiple-choice questions, eliminate any answers that you know are incorrect—this will narrow the field of choices remaining to you. When completing a matching exercise, first go through the entire list of items, matching all the items that you know for sure. Then study any items that remain. Read essay questions carefully so that you know precisely what you are being asked to write. Create an outline of the main ideas and supporting details that you plan to include in your essay. Keep your answer clear and brief, but be sure that you cover all the necessary points.

HOW TO TAKE A TEST

1. **Prepare beforehand.** This vitally important step involves more than studying and reviewing the information prior to the test. It also means being well rested and mentally focused on the day of the test.

2. **Follow directions.** Remember to read all test instructions carefully. Listen closely if the directions are oral rather than written. Ask for clarification as needed.

3. **Preview the test.** Skim the entire test and judge how much time you have to complete each section. Try to anticipate which areas of the test will be the most difficult for you and stick to your time schedule.

4. **Concentrate on the test.** Do not "watch the clock," but do stay aware of the time. If you do not know the answer to a question, move on to the next question. It is best to answer as many questions as you can within the allowed time.

5. **Review your answers.** If time permits, revise answers you were unsure of and answer those you skipped. Review your essay to catch and correct any errors in spelling, punctuation, or grammar.

PRACTICING YOUR SKILL

To practice your skill, answer the following questions.

1. What can you do to improve your chances on multiple-choice questions?

2. Why is it important to read essay questions carefully?

3. Why is it important to preview the test before you begin?

4. What should you do if you do not know the answer to a question? Why?

5. What should you do if you find that you have time left at the end of the test?

TAKING A TEST   SKILL WORKSHEET

APPLYING THE SKILL I

This section of the worksheet will help you to evaluate your test-preparation skills. First, read the statements below. Then, circle the number to the right of each statement to identify your strength or weakness in that particular area.

	Strong	Fairly Strong	Average	Fairly Weak	Weak
1. I make sure that my study habits are consistent.	5	4	3	2	1
2. I allow myself enough time to review the material before a test.	5	4	3	2	1
3. I get plenty of rest the night before a test.	5	4	3	2	1
4. On the day of the test, I stay mentally focused.	5	4	3	2	1

I can improve my test-preparation skills by _____

_____

_____

_____.

APPLYING THE SKILL II

This section of the worksheet will help you to evaluate your test-taking skills. To complete the section, follow the directions given above in Applying the Skill I.

	Strong	Fairly Strong	Average	Fairly Weak	Weak
1. I read all test instructions carefully.	5	4	3	2	1
2. I preview tests before I begin.	5	4	3	2	1
3. I try to judge how much time I will need to complete each test section.	5	4	3	2	1
4. I stay aware of the time.	5	4	3	2	1
5. If I do not know an answer, I move on to the next question.	5	4	3	2	1
6. I return to and work on questions I skipped or were unsure of.	5	4	3	2	1
7. I review my essays for spelling, punctuation, and grammar errors.	5	4	3	2	1

I can improve my test-taking skills by _____

_____

_____

_____.

CONDUCTING AN INTERVIEW   SKILL LESSON

People who were present at a particular situation or event often are the best source of information about it. For this reason, social scientists often conduct interviews with individuals who have witnessed or participated in historical events. These interviews, which also are referred to as oral histories, are an excellent way to gain firsthand knowledge of an event. Applying the following guidelines will help you to become a truly effective interviewer.

HOW TO CONDUCT AN INTERVIEW

1. **Identify the situation or event you want to learn about.** When choosing a topic, keep in mind that the event you want to learn about must be recent enough to ensure that some of the people who were present at the event are still living. For example, it would today be impossible to find people who lived through the Civil War, but it would be possible to interview people from World War II.

2. **Identify the individual you want to interview.** Determine what categories of people can supply you with firsthand information about your topic. If you want to interview an individual who was involved in World War II, for instance, you could interview a World War II veteran, a former military nurse who worked in a war zone, a former military or civilian prisoner of war, or a person who lived in Europe or Asia during World War II.

3. **Research your topic.** Conduct library research to gather information on the circumstances surrounding the event. Do as much research as possible, but focus your research on information relevant to the individual you will be interviewing. For example, if you are going to interview a woman who was living in the United States during World War II, you might want to focus your research on the ways that women in the United States contributed to the war effort.

4. **Set up the interview.** Contact the individual you wish to interview, and introduce yourself. Explain the purpose of the interview, then establish a convenient time and place to conduct the interview. If you wish to tape-record or video-record the interview, remember that you must first seek and obtain the permission of the interviewee (the person to be interviewed).

5. **Prepare your questions.** You will want to ask open-ended questions, which are questions that require more than a "yes" or "no" response. For instance, you might ask "What was it like to grow up during a time of such political conflict?" rather than "Was it difficult to be a child during the war years?" Using open-ended questions will allow you to obtain a much fuller and richer picture of the event being discussed than would simple yes-no questions. Prepare at least seven such questions you will want to ask the interviewee. Depending on the person you interview, you may not need to ask all of these questions, but you should at least be prepared to do so.

6. **Conduct the interview.** Begin the interview with your most important questions. Allow the interviewee to go beyond your specific line of questioning, but remember to keep the interview going in the right direction. If you do not understand a statement or an idea, ask the interviewee for clarification. If you need additional information about an answer, ask several more in-depth questions, but stick to the point. Write down only important information and do not get too involved in taking notes. Even if you tape-record or video-record the interview, be sure to have some paper and a pencil handy so that you can jot down additional questions that occur to you during the interview.

7. **Act in a professional manner.** If there are topics or issues that the interviewee would rather not discuss, respect his or her wishes and pursue another line of questioning. Remember that people

have the right to refuse to answer a question. In addition, an interviewee might later ask you not to use certain portions of the interview. Again, respect his or her wishes in this regard. Interviewees have the right to expect that you will keep information confidential if they desire it. Keep in mind that they also have the right to end the interview at any point during the session. While this may mean that you will have to find someone else to interview, do not try to pressure your interviewee into continuing the session.

8. **Do a follow-up.** At the close of the interview, ask if you may call the person for additional information if needed. Be sure to thank the person for his or her time. Follow up your expression of appreciation with a handwritten thank-you note.

9. **Analyze the interview.** As soon as possible after the close of the interview, while the session is still fresh in your mind, write a summary. Pay particular attention to the kinds of information the interviewee emphasized and which statements represented his or her overall views. As you write your summary, ask yourself the following questions: Have I introduced the interviewee and the topic of the interview? Have I put my interviewee and my interview topic in their historical and social contexts? Have I presented a vivid yet factual description of the event or experience from my interviewee's point of view?

PRACTICING YOUR SKILL

To practice your skill, answer the following questions.

1. What important point should you keep in mind when choosing a topic for your interview?

2. What should be the focus of library research you do to gather background material on an event?

3. What must you first do if you wish to tape-record or video-record an interview?

4. Why is it important to prepare open-ended rather than yes-no questions?

5. Why is it important to have paper and a pencil handy even if you plan to tape-record or video-record an interview?

6. What rights do all interviewees have during the course of an interview?

7. Why is it important to write a summary of the interview as soon as possible after the interview is over?

8. What three questions should you keep in mind as you write your summary of the interview?

CONDUCTING AN INTERVIEW

SKILL WORKSHEET

APPLYING THE SKILL I

This section of the worksheet will help you in your preparation for conducting an interview. Before your interview, complete each of the items below.

1. Choose one of the following general topics to serve as the focus of your interview.

_____ **a.** a war

_____ **b.** a social movement

_____ **c.** the immigrant experience

_____ **d.** a country's political system

_____ **e.** a country's educational system

_____ **f.** a country's health care system

_____ **g.** the adolescent experience

_____ **h.** family life

_____ **i.** a natural disaster, such as a hurricane

_____ **j.** other (teacher approved): _____

The specific focus of my interview will be _____

_____.

2. Identify four categories of people who can supply you with firsthand information about your topic.

a. _____

b. _____

c. _____

d. _____

3. Prepare seven open-ended questions to ask your interviewee.

a. _____

b. _____

c. _____

d. _____

e. _____

f. _____

g. _____

APPLYING THE SKILL II

This section of the worksheet will help you to analyze your interview. After you have conducted the interview, complete each of the items below.

1. Topic of the interview: _____

2. Name of interviewee: _____

3. Reasons I chose this person as my interviewee: _____

_____

4. Date of the interview: _____

5. Location of the interview: _____

6. This interview was (check one) _____ tape-recorded.   _____ video-recorded.   _____ neither.

7. Kinds of information emphasized by interviewee: _____

_____

_____

8. Interviewee's most significant statements: _____

_____

_____

9. Summary of my interview: _____

_____

_____

_____

_____

_____

_____

_____

_____

_____

_____

_____

_____

ANALYZING TABLES   SKILL LESSON

In all areas of Social Studies, statistical data often are presented in the form of tables. Statistical tables display numerical information in a format that is easy to read and understand. Tables most often are used to show the changes in numbers over time. For example, a table can be used to show population changes in the nation's major cities over a certain period of time. In a table, statistics usually are listed in columns. Learning to analyze tables can give you access to a great deal of information about particular topics.

HOW TO ANALYZE TABLES

1. **Determine the table's subject.** Read the title of the table to determine the table's subject and purpose.
2. **Examine the headings.** Tables generally have two sets of headings. These headings tell you how the data has been organized, or into what categories it has been divided. Each vertical column has its own heading. A heading also appears to the left of each horizontal row. Study the headings, and make sure you know to which column or row each heading refers. Also make sure you know what each heading means before you try to read the table.
3. **Analyze the information.** Determine what units of measurement are used in the table. The unit of measurement usually is shown in the table title or in the column headings. Common units include percentages, dollars, hundreds, thousands, and rates per 1,000 (such as 6 in every 1,000). Also note the time periods covered in the table and the categories of informational data being presented. To locate specific data on a table, look down a vertical column and across a horizontal row. Where the column and row meet is where you will find the information you need.
4. **Put the data to use.** Look for relationships among the data, such as any similarities, differences, and trends. Trends in the data can be determined by reading down each column or across each row. Draw conclusions based on the data.

PRACTICING YOUR SKILL

To practice your skill, examine the table below and then answer the questions that follow.

FEMALE LABOR FORCE PARTICIPATION RATES BY MARITAL STATUS, 1960–1994				
	Participation Rate (in percents)			
Year	Total	Single	Married[1]	Other[2]
1960	37.7	58.6	31.9	41.6
1965	39.3	54.5	34.9	40.7
1970	43.3	56.8	40.5	40.3
1975	46.3	59.8	44.3	40.1
1980	51.5	64.6	49.9	43.6
1985	54.5	66.6	53.8	45.1
1990	57.5	66.9	58.4	47.2
1994	58.8	66.7	60.7	47.5

[1] Husband present.
[2] Widowed, divorced, or separated.
Source: *Statistical Abstract of the United States, 1995*, p. 405.

1. What is the purpose of the table?
2. What do the column headings and the headings on the left tell you about the data?
3. What units of measurement are used in the table?
4. What conclusions can you draw about the data?

ANALYZING TABLES

SKILL WORKSHEET

APPLYING THE SKILL

To apply your skill, examine the table below and then answer the questions that follow.

		Urban		Rural	
URBAN AND RURAL POPULATION OF THE UNITED STATES, 1900–1990					
Year	**Total Population**	**Population**	**% of Total Pop.**	**Population**	**% of Total Pop.**
1900	75,994,575	30,093,852	39.6	45,900,723	60.4
1910	91,972,266	41,939,353	45.6	50,032,913	54.4
1920	105,710,620	54,123,837	51.2	51,586,783	48.8
1930	122,775,046	68,876,801	56.1	53,898,245	43.9
1940	131,669,275	74,393,140	56.5	57,276,135	43.5
1950	150,697,361	96,446,311	64.0	54,251,050	36.0
1960	179,323,175	125,346,899	69.9	53,976,276	30.1
1970	203,302,031	149,426,993	73.5	53,875,038	26.5
1980	226,545,805	166,964,258	73.7	59,581,547	26.3
1990	248,709,873	187,029,825	75.2	61,680,048	24.8

Source: *The Universal Almanac, 1996*, p. 292.

1. What is the table's purpose?_____

2. What do the column headings indicate about the data?_____

_____

3. What units of measurement are being used? _____

4. What was the total population of the United States in 1910? in 1940? in 1990? _____

_____

5. What percentage of the U.S. population lived in rural areas in 1930? in 1950? in 1970?

_____

6. In what year did the urban population reach nearly 42 million? What percentage of the total population for that year does this figure represent?

_____

7. If the column titled "Total Population" were not included in the table, how could you use the data in the table to find total U.S. population for each of the decades shown?

_____

8. What is the source of the data used in the table?_____

9. What conclusions can be drawn from the data?_____

_____

CONDUCTING A DEBATE   **SKILL LESSON**

Many topics and issues in your Social Studies classes lend themselves to debate. A debate is a formal competition between two opposing teams to determine which team is more skilled in speaking and reasoning. The two teams publicly argue an issue in a well-organized and efficient manner, appealing to logic and reason rather than to emotion. Success in a debate is determined by the skill of the debaters in presenting and supporting their ideas, not by any truths about the topic, or proposition, under debate. Applying the following guidelines will help you to organize and conduct a debate.

HOW TO CONDUCT A DEBATE

Before debating some issues, actions, and topics in Social Studies, you will need to become familiar with contemporary issues, such as crime, homelessness, and capital punishment. Other debate opportunities will require you to use your historical imagination to argue issues and actions from the past. For example, if you are studying World War II, you may wish to debate whether or not President Truman should have dropped the atomic bomb on Japan to force the nation's surrender.

No matter their focus, however, all classroom debates involve the following three major stages: preparing for the debate, holding the debate, and evaluating the debate. Each of these stages can be further divided into more specific steps and tasks. The guidelines for each of these three stages, which follow below, can help you to improve your debating skills and produce more reasoned and persuasive arguments.

PREPARING FOR THE DEBATE

1. **Select the teams.** Each of the two debate teams should have at least two or three members, although the size of the team may vary depending on the particular topic to be debated or the format that will be used. You may have the opportunity to choose the other members of your team, or your teacher may choose your teammates for you. In either case, remind your teammates that cooperation is one of the keys to winning a debate.

2. **State the proposition.** A proposition is a statement or resolution that your team and the opposing team first research and then discuss in the debate. The proposition most often is stated as a resolution, a formal statement of opinion. Take care to avoid words that appeal only to emotion, that are unclear, or that favor one team over the other. Keep in mind that one of the teams—called the affirmative team—must defend the proposition. The opposing team—known as the negative team—must speak against the proposition. State the proposition in the affirmative to place the burden of proof on the affirmative team. The following are sample propositions that are relevant to Social Studies. Note that these propositions focus on both contemporary and historical themes.

SAMPLE PROPOSITIONS

- **Resolved:** Capital punishment should be abolished in the United States.
- **Resolved:** The United States should join the League of Nations.
- **Resolved:** The U.S. government should provide medical insurance to Americans who cannot afford it.
- **Resolved:** President Richard Nixon should have faced legal prosecution for his role in the Watergate scandal.
- **Resolved:** An amendment to balance the federal budget should be added to the U.S. Constitution.

---

3. **Research your topic.** Once you have selected your team and stated your proposition, organize your team. Make sure that each member of the team participates in researching the issues surrounding the proposition. Remind your teammates that it is the strength of your arguments and the clarity of your presentation that will determine your team's success.

4. **Prepare a brief.** When you and your teammates have completed your research, organize your information in a brief. A brief is an orderly arrangement of complete sentences that state the main points of your arguments. Be sure to present your arguments in a clear, concise, and logical manner. During your research you will undoubtedly uncover a number of points over which you expect a clash of ideas and opinions with the opposing team. These points are known as issues and should be included in your brief. State each issue as a question that can be answered either yes or no. Answer each question, including reasons for your answer.

5. **Outline your brief.** Write an outline of your brief on index cards. Keep the information on the cards as brief as possible, and do not read them word for word to the class. Rather, use the cards only as a means of organizing your thoughts during the actual debate. Review and revise your arguments following the opposing team's presentation.

HOLDING THE DEBATE

6. **Present your arguments.** In the first part of the debate, known as the constructive speeches, each team presents its arguments for or against the proposition. Members of each team speak alternately, starting with the affirmative team. Note that each constructive speech is limited to eight minutes.

7. **Use the intermission wisely.** Following the last constructive speech, there is an intermission. Use this time to evaluate your team's position in the debate and to get ready for the next round of speeches. Talk with your teammates, and formulate a plan for further action. Determine both how you will try to disprove your opponents' arguments and the order in which you will speak. If the opposing team has raised issues not covered in your speeches, examine your research notes for information to use in your further arguments.

8. **Present your rebuttal.** The rebuttal is the second part of the debate. During the rebuttal, each team refutes, or attempts to disprove, the arguments presented by the opposing team during the constructive speeches. Members of the opposing teams speak alternately, starting with the negative team. Each rebuttal speech is limited to four minutes. Be prepared to refute your opponents' arguments, attacking their main points first. Restate their arguments clearly and fairly, quoting them exactly whenever possible. Refute each argument by showing, through evidence you have researched and collected, that the argument is misleading, unproved, or irrelevant.

EVALUATING THE DEBATE

9. **Seek feedback.** After the debate has ended, have the class vote on which team presented the most convincing argument. Tally the results on the chalkboard. Then ask the members of the class to discuss the degree to which their support of or opposition to the proposition was influenced by the debate. Use these comments as the basis of a class discussion on the topic suggested by the proposition.

PRACTICING YOUR SKILL

To practice your skill, answer the following questions.
1. In a debate, what is the role of the affirmative team? What is the role of the negative team?
2. What is a brief? Why is it important?
3. Which team begins the constructive speeches? What is the time limit for each speech?
4. What happens during the rebuttal part of the debate? What is the time limit for each rebuttal speech?

CONDUCTING A DEBATE **SKILL WORKSHEET**

APPLYING THE SKILL I

This section of the worksheet will help you in your preparation for a debate. Before your debate, complete each of the items below.

1. My debate team has a total of _____ members.

2. My teammates are _____.

3. My debate proposition is _____

_____.

4. My team is the (check one) _____ affirmative team. _____ negative team.

5. The issues and topics researched by my team include_____

_____

_____.

6. I anticipate that my team and the opposing team will clash over the issues of_____

_____

_____.

APPLYING THE SKILL II

In the space provided below, on a separate sheet of paper, or a computer, write your debate brief.

BRIEF

_____

_____

_____

_____

_____

_____

_____

_____

_____

Applying the Skill III

This section of the worksheet will help to you evaluate your debate-preparation skills. First, read the statements below. Then, circle the number to the right of each statement to identify your strength or weakness in that particular area.

	Strong	Fairly Strong	Average	Fairly Weak	Weak
1. I had a clear understanding of the debate proposition.	5	4	3	2	1
2. I fully participated in the research process.	5	4	3	2	1
3. I wrote my brief in a clear, concise, and logical manner.	5	4	3	2	1
4. I prepared a well-organized, concise outline of my brief.	5	4	3	2	1
5. I worked well with my teammates.	5	4	3	2	1

I can improve my debate-preparation skills by_____

_____

_____

_____ .

Applying the Skill IV

This section of the worksheet will help you to evaluate your debating skills. To complete the section, follow the directions given above in Applying the Skill III.

	Strong	Fairly Strong	Average	Fairly Weak	Weak
1. I spoke loudly and clearly enough to be heard by the entire audience.	5	4	3	2	1
2. I used my index cards only to organize my thoughts.	5	4	3	2	1
3. My constructive speech was well-organized, logical, and persuasive.	5	4	3	2	1
4. I used the intermission time wisely.	5	4	3	2	1
5. My rebuttal speech successfully refuted my opponents' arguments.	5	4	3	2	1

I can improve my debate-preparation skills by_____

_____

_____

_____ .

IDENTIFYING THE MAIN IDEA
SKILL LESSON

1. Having questions in mind as you read a selection will help you to focus your reading.

2. Following the trail of facts provided in a selection may lead to a conclusion that expresses a main idea.

3. The focus of the paragraph is on religious conflicts in England. The main idea is expressed in the last sentence: there was no "truly Protestant church" in England, and this fact caused great distress for the Pilgrims.

4. Details about King Henry VIII and the creation of the Anglican Church provide a background to the religious conflicts and lend support to the paragraph's main idea.

SKILL WORKSHEET
APPLYING THE SKILL I

1. The main idea of the paragraph is the Pilgrims' need to search for religious freedom.

2. Details about life in the Netherlands and the Pilgrim leader's views about this new life support the main idea.

3. The main idea of the paragraph on page 5—that the Pilgrims desired a more Protestant church—provides the cause for the main idea of the paragraph about the Pilgrims—that they had to search for religious freedom. Students' statements should reflect an understanding of the reasons the Pilgrims sought permission to settle in Virginia.

APPLYING THE SKILL II

Students should write a paragraph on a topic about which they have a strong basic knowledge. They should be able to identify the main idea of the paragraph and the details that support the main idea.

IDENTIFYING CAUSE AND EFFECT
SKILL LESSON

1. **Cause**
   Britain incurs a huge debt while fighting the French and Indian War.
   Effect
   Parliament levies taxes on the colonies.

2. **Cause**
   Britain incurs a huge debt while fighting the French and Indian War.
   Effect/Cause
   Parliament levies taxes on the colonies.
   Effect
   Colonists protest taxation without representation.

SKILL WORKSHEET
APPLYING THE SKILL I

1. It is sometimes necessary to judge what is a cause or an effect because writers do not always state the link between cause and effect.

2. Three things that should be checked when looking for complex relationships are whether there were other causes of a given effect beyond the immediate cause, whether a cause had multiple effects, and whether these effects themselves caused further events.

3. Examples of "cause" words or phrases may include *instigated* and *motivated*. Examples of "effect" words or phrases may include *became* and *derived from*. Accept any reasonable answers.

APPLYING THE SKILL II

1. a
2. b
3. b
4. b
5. a
6. a

STUDYING PRIMARY AND SECONDARY SOURCES
SKILL LESSON

1. The passage is a primary source because it was written by Washington himself as he was about to leave office.

2. The basic message of the passage is that the United States should isolate itself politically from the other nations of the world.

3. The speech was intended for the American people.

4. Washington, as the first president of the United States, was in a unique position both to make U.S. foreign policy and to influence the foreign policy of his successors.

SKILL WORKSHEET
APPLYING THE SKILL I

1. P
2. P
3. S
4. P
5. P
6. S
7. P
8. S
9. P
10. P

APPLYING THE SKILL II

1. The Declaration of Independence is a primary source because it is an original document containing firsthand information.

2. The purpose of the first paragraph is to provide justification for the separation of the American colonies from Great Britain.

3. All people are entitled to life, liberty, and the pursuit of happiness.

4. If a government abuses its power, the people have the right to do away with that government.

BUILDING YOUR VOCABULARY
SKILL LESSON

1. Context refers to the other words or sentences that surround a specific word in a paragraph or sentence. The context can provide clues to a word's meaning by supplying either a familiar synonym or an example.

2. The dictionary contains pronunciation guides and definitions of words.

3. Using a thesaurus to find synonyms might help familiarize you with new or unusual words.

4. Using new words is the best way to master them.

5. Students should list and define any new vocabulary words in the chapter they read and then check their definitions against those in a dictionary. They should also create a plan to commit those words to memory.

SKILL WORKSHEET
APPLYING THE SKILL I

1. e
2. d
3. f
4. a
5. c
6. b

APPLYING THE SKILL II

1. ecosystem
2. veto
3. utopia
4. electors
5. depression
6. carpetbaggers
7. segregation
8. urban renewal

DISTINGUISHING FACT FROM OPINION
SKILL LESSON

1. The loaded words in the sentence are *dedicated, hardworking,* and *successfully.* These words might influence people to look favorably on the candidate.

2. Journalists would first have to verify the accuracy of the statements contained in the flier. If their accuracy is verified, the following statements can be considered facts: city taxes have been increased four times over a 10-year period; 25 percent of public buses do not operate during rush hour; more than 200 of the city's older citizens are waiting to participate in city-run programs; Ortega has served on the school board for more than 10 years.

SKILL WORKSHEET
APPLYING THE SKILL I

1. F
2. O
3. O
4. F
5. O
6. O
7. F
8. F
9. O
10. F

APPLYING THE SKILL II

All factual statements should contain information that can be verified. All opinions should be based on personal beliefs.

FORMING GENERALIZATIONS
SKILL LESSON

1. It is important that all of the evidence lead to the same conclusion because if any of the facts do not fit, the generalization will be incorrect.

2. A generalization can be considered valid if it is broad enough to take into account all of the facts but does not make claims that the facts do not support.

3. Students may say that the school is closed or that it is a weekend or holiday.

4. The generalization is "Changes in technology affect the kinds of jobs available to workers."

SKILL WORKSHEET
APPLYING THE SKILL I

1. b
2. c
3. a

APPLYING THE SKILL II

1. One generalization that may be formed is that the Great Depression was a time of enormous hardship for many Americans.

2. One generalization that may be formed is that most wealth in the United States is owned by a minority of the people.

DOING LIBRARY RESEARCH
SKILL LESSON

1. Nonfiction books are classified by the Dewey decimal system and the Library of Congress system.

2. The card catalog provides a book's call number, title, author, subjects, and publication information.

3. Reference books that contain information about geography include encyclopedias, specialized dictionaries, gazetteers, and atlases.

4. To locate the most recent coverage of a political or social issue, you would look in almanacs, encyclopedia yearbooks, and periodical indexes.

SKILL WORKSHEET
APPLYING THE SKILL I

1. almanac
2. biographical dictionary; encyclopedia
3. encyclopedia
4. *Readers' Guide to Periodical Literature*
5. atlas; gazetteer
6. gazetteer
7. biographical dictionary; encyclopedia
8. historical dictionary

APPLYING THE SKILL II

1. The title of the book is *The Student's Guide to Fascinating U.S. History Facts.*

2. The author of the book is John Doe.

3. The book was published in 1997.

4. The publisher of the book is the Superior Publishing Company.

5. The book contains 436 pages.

6. The book's call number is 973.02 DOE.

CREATING AN OUTLINE
SKILL LESSON

1. There are four levels of headings included in the outline.

2. The two main ideas contained in the outline are the fact that the Republicans supported westward expansion and that President Jefferson negotiated with France.

3. The fact that France regained control of Louisiana caused concern for the United States because it threatened U.S. trade and could prove to be a barrier to U.S. expansion westward.

4. The two reasons why France decided to sell Louisiana to the United States are that Napoleon failed to build an empire in the Americas and that he needed money for his war plans.

SKILL WORKSHEET
APPLYING THE SKILL I

1. I. Introduction/purpose
2. II. Who lives in poverty?
3.   A. Unskilled workers
4.   B. Racial and ethnic groups
5.   C. Older Americans
6.   D. Single-parent families
7. III. Effects of poverty
8.   A. Health
9.   B. Education
10.   C. Self-esteem
11. IV. Programs to ease poverty
12.   A. Government programs
13.   B. Volunteer programs
14. V. Summary/conclusions

APPLYING THE SKILL II

Student outlines will vary but should include the main ideas and supporting details contained within the subsection of the chapter. Be sure that students use the proper outline structure and that outlines contain at least two levels of headings.

WRITING ABOUT SOCIAL STUDIES
SKILL LESSON

1. The factor that should most affect how and what you write is your purpose for writing—different purposes for writing require different forms, tones, and contents.

2. It is important to consider the intended audience because the content and style of writing must be shaped to fit that audience.

3. When editing the first draft of a writing assignment, you should revise, reorganize, and refine sentences, and delete unnecessary or unrelated words, sentences, or paragraphs.

4. It is important to prepare a neat final version of a writing assignment because appearance can affect the way work is perceived by others.

SKILL WORKSHEET
APPLYING THE SKILL I–IV

Students should complete all four stages in the writing process: prewriting, writing the first draft, evaluating and revising the draft, and proofreading and publishing. Offer clarification of the tasks involved in each stage as necessary, and make sure that students complete the checklists. After students have completed all sections of the worksheet, you may wish to have them discuss how working through the four stages has affected their views about the writing experience.

TAKING A TEST
SKILL LESSON

1. You can improve your chances on multiple-choice questions by eliminating any answers that you know are incorrect.

2. It is important to read essay questions carefully so that you know precisely what you are being asked to write.

3. It is important to preview the test before you begin so that you can judge approximately how much time will be required for each section of the test and anticipate which areas of the test will prove most difficult.

4. If you do not know the answer to a question, you should move on to the next question; it is best to answer as many questions as possible within the allowed time.

5. If you have time left at the end of a test, you should revise questions you were unsure of and answer any you skipped.

SKILL WORKSHEET
APPLYING THE SKILL I–II

Encourage students to make an honest evaluation of their test-preparation and test-taking skills and to think carefully about what they can do to improve these skills. Challenge students to act on the improvements they suggest for themselves and later to discuss how these improvements have affected their test-preparation and test-taking experiences.

CONDUCTING AN INTERVIEW
SKILL LESSON

1. When choosing a topic, it is important that the event be recent enough to ensure that some of the people who were present at the event are still living.

2. The focus of the library research should be on information relevant to the person who will be interviewed.

3. If you wish to tape-record or video-record an interview, you must first obtain the interviewee's permission to do so.

4. Open-ended questions obtain more information and a much fuller and richer picture of an event than do yes-no questions

5. Having paper and a pencil handy during tape-recorded or video-recorded interviews allows you to write down any additional questions that you might want to ask.

6. All interviewees have the right to refuse to answer a question, the right to ask the interviewer to keep certain information confiden-

tial, and the right to end the interview whenever they wish.

7. It is important to write a summary as soon as possible after the interview is over to ensure that it is fresh in your mind when you write.

8. The three questions you should keep in mind are as follows: Have I introduced the interviewee and the topic of the interview? Have I put my interviewee and my interview topic in their historical and social contexts? and Have I presented a vivid yet factual description of the event or experience from my interviewee's point of view?

SKILL WORKSHEET
APPLYING THE SKILL I

Make sure that students complete all items on the page and that they have your approval for topics other than those listed. You may wish to have students work in pairs to conduct the interviews—one student to ask the questions and the other student to take notes during the interview. Both students can share in the library research, question writing, and other preinterview tasks.

APPLYING THE SKILL II

Make sure that students complete all items on the page, even if they have worked in pairs to conduct the interview. You may wish to ask volunteers to read aloud the summaries of their interviews. After students have completed their analyses, have them discuss what they learned both about their interview topics and about the interview process. Also ask students to explain why conducting interviews is an important part of the research process.

ANALYZING TABLES
SKILL LESSON

1. The purpose of the table is to show female labor force participation rates by marital status for the years 1960 to 1994.

2. The column headings indicate that the data show total female participation in the labor force and female labor force participation by marital status. The headings on the left show the years under consideration.

3. Percentages are the units of measurement used in the table.

4. Students should notice that total female labor force participation has increased over the years, that the labor force participation of women in all marital status categories has increased over the years, and that single women tend to have the highest rate of labor force participation.

SKILL WORKSHEET
APPLYING THE SKILL

1. The purpose of the table is to show the urban and rural population of the United States from 1900 to 1990.

2. The column headings indicate that the data show the total population of the United States and the number and percentage of the population that live in urban and rural areas.

3. Percentages are the units of measurement used in the table.

4. The total population of the United States in 1910 was 91,972,266; in 1940 it was 131,669,275; in 1990 it was 248,709,873.

5. The rural population in 1930 was 43.9 percent; in 1950 it was 36.0 percent; in 1970 it was 26.5 percent.

6. The urban population reached nearly 42 million in 1910. The figure of nearly 42 million represents 45.6 percent of the total population for 1910.

7. You could add the urban and rural population numbers for each decade to find the total U.S. population figure.

8. The source of the data used in the table is *The Universal Almanac, 1996.*

9. Students should conclude that the total U.S. population has been increasing steadily over the years, that the percentage of the U.S. population living in urban areas has been increasing over the years, and that while the number of people living in rural areas generally has been increasing over time, the rural population as a percentage of total U.S. population has been decreasing. Ask students to speculate on what these trends tell us about the probable urban and rural population of the United States in the year 2000.

CONDUCTING A DEBATE
SKILL LESSON

1. The role of the affirmative team is to defend the proposition. The role of the negative team is to speak against the proposition.

2. A brief is an orderly arrangement of complete sentences that state the main points of arguments in a debate. It also contains questions and answers about anticipated issues. The brief is important because it serves as a guide during the debate process.

3. The affirmative team begins the constructive speeches part of the debate. Each constructive speech is limited to eight minutes.

4. During the rebuttal part of the debate, each team refutes the arguments which were presented by the opposing team during the constructive speeches. Members of opposing teams speak alternately, starting with the negative team. The time limit for each rebuttal speech is four minutes.

SKILL WORKSHEET
APPLYING THE SKILL I

Make sure that students complete all items in the section. You may want to assign debate propositions to teams of students or have the teams decide on a proposition from among the topics being studied in class. If you allow the teams to choose their own propositions, remind them to obtain your approval of their propositions before they begin their research. Also make sure that students understand the roles of the affirmative team and the negative team.

APPLYING THE SKILL II

Remind students of the purpose of a brief and that their briefs should contain complete sentences that state the main points of their arguments. Also remind students that the outline of the brief, to be written on index cards, should contain only the main points of their arguments and should be used only to refresh their memories. Offer help as needed to those students having difficulty anticipating potential issues in the debate.

APPLYING THE SKILL III–IV

Encourage students to make an honest evaluation of their debate-preparation and debating skills and to think carefully about what they can do to improve these skills. Remind students that although a debate is a team effort, every individual on the team has a vital role to play in ensuring that the team is successful.